Volleyball

Bernie Blackall

D0230856

Heinemann
LIBRARY

First published in Great Britain by Heinemann Library, Halley Court, Jordan Hill,
Oxford OX2 8EJ, a division of Reed Educational and Professional Publishing Ltd.

Heinemann is a registered trademark of Reed Educational & Professional
Publishing Limited.

02 01 00 99
10 9 8 7 6 5 4 3 2 1

OXFORD   MELBOURNE   AUCKLAND
BLANTYRE   IBADAN   JOHANNESBURG   GABORONE
PORTSMOUTH NH (USA)   CHICAGO

Series cover and text design by Karen Young
Paged by Jo Pritchard
Cover by Smarty-pants Design
Cover photographs by: Sport. The Library/Jeff Crow (left); Mike Liles
Edited by Jane Pearson
Illustrations by Vasja Koman
Picture research by Kirsty Grant and Lara Artis
Production by Cindy Smith
Film separations by Impact Printing Pty Ltd
Printed in Hong Kong by Wing King Tong

British Library Cataloguing in Publication Data
Blackall, Bernie
Volleyball. – (Top Sport)
1.Volleyball – Juvenile literature 2.Volleyball – Miscellanea – Juvenile literature
I.Title
796.3'25

ISBN 0 431 03658 6
This title is also available in a hardback library edition (ISBN 0 431 03653 5)

Acknowledgements
The Publishers would like to thank the following for permission to reproduce
photographs: Coo-ee Picture Library: pp 11 (top), 20. Mike Liles: pp 11 (bottom),
19 (top), 23 (left). Empics Ltd: pp 6, 7. Sporting Pix: Greg Ford, p 26; Bob Thomas,
p 17. Sport. The Library: p 6; Jeff Crow pp 14, 23 (right); Andrew Freeman p 27.
Sydney Freelance: pp 5, 10, 19 (bottom). Volleyball Hall of Fame, Holyoke,
Massachusetts: p 8. YMCA of the USA Archives, University of Minnesota Libraries:
p 9.

Special thanks to Volleyball Victoria, Craig Smith, Head coach, Victorian Institute
of Sport, Simone Brown, Narelle Lloyd and Peter Jones of Volleyball Victoria,
Ana Paulic, Australian Volleyball Federation and Kirk Bizley.

Every effort has been made to contact copyright holders of any material reproduced
in this book. Any omissions will be rectified in subsequent printings if notice is given
to the Publisher.

Any words appearing in the text in bold, **like this**, are explained in the Glossary.

Contents

About volleyball

Volleyball is an Olympic sport with an estimated 250 million players worldwide. It is a team game played on a **court** divided by a high net. There are six players per team and each team aims to hit the ball over the net to land on its opponent's court.

Play begins with the ball being served by a **back-court** player who stands behind the back boundary line, called the end line, of the court. After the ball is served over the net, each team is allowed three touches before the ball is hit back over the net. They must not let the ball touch the ground on their side of the court or they will give the other team a point or lose the serve.

Only the serving team can score a point. When the serving team wins a **rally**, a point is added to its score and the team continues to **serve**. When the receiving team wins a rally, there is no change to the score but it wins the right to serve.

A **set** is won by the first team to score 15 points – as long as the team has a two point lead. The match winner is the first team to score three sets.

Played at elite level, volleyball is a very dynamic and spectacular sport.

With the official introduction of beach volleyball at the 1996 Olympic Games, a new dimension has been added to the game. Rules have been modified for the new two-player-per-side format.

British Highlights

The EVA

The English Volleyball Association (EVA) was formed in 1972. It replaced the English Volleyball Association of Great Britain and Northern Ireland which had previously been the body in charge of volleyball. The EVA is working hard to raise the standard and profile of volleyball and to encourage more participation in the sport.

Volleyball clubs

There are over 400 senior clubs and 400 junior/school clubs that are members of the EVA and there are over 1,800 teams that take part in various competitions. A survey held in 1997 showed that 1.9 million children in Britain play volleyball at least once a year.

Volleyball is an Olympic sport. These teams are competing at the Atlanta Olympic Games in 1996.

Beach volleyball

There are also beach volleyball clubs that take part in competitions which run from May until September. The first national junior beach championships were held in 1996 and for the seniors there are five Grand Prix events that lead up to the British Beach Open Championships. The EVA even organises volleyball for disabled people.

British players

Two British men (Matt Jones and Marcus Russell) play professional volleyball in Belgium. British players have had the most success in beach volleyball – Amanda Glover and Audrey Cooper finished 9th in the Atlanta Olympic Games.

Amanda Glover in action playing beach volleyball at Atlanta in 1996.

The ball must not touch the ground during play.

History of volleyball

The original Holyoke volleyball team. William Morgan is standing at the left.

Volleyball originated in Holyoke, Massachusetts in 1895. William G. Morgan, a young instructor at the Young Men's Christian Association (YMCA), had introduced basketball to his middle-aged members but they found it too fast and too demanding.

He decided to create a game which involved less running, and which could be played on a smaller area.

Mintonette

Morgan adapted the rules and the equipment from several games already in existence. From tennis he borrowed the net and strung it at a height of two metres across the middle of a basketball court. He used the soft bladder of a basketball as it was soft and light allowing players to volley the ball without pain or injury. Morgan's new game was called mintonette.

The basic rule of mintonette was that the ball must not touch the ground. A point was scored to the opposition when it did. Players were required to volley the ball back over the net – they were not allowed to catch it. Teams consisted of nine players each – in three rows of three. Team **rotation** on the court ensured that all players took turns in all positions on the court during a game.

Volleyball was a popular outdoor game in the American countryside. This game is being played in Maryland in 1911.

A new name

At the YMCA conference in 1896, the name volleyball was adopted because every hit was a **volley**. Teams were reduced to six players, the court was enlarged slightly and a new, lighter, leather ball was introduced.

Volleyball spread quickly throughout the USA – largely through the YMCA network. In 1918 the game was introduced into Western Europe by American troops. From here it spread around the world. It became very popular in Japan and Russia – countries that still dominate international competition.

In Paris in 1947 the International Volleyball Federation (Federatione Internationale de Volleyball – FIDV) was formed. It remains the sport's governing body. The first World Championships for men were held in 1949 and for women in 1952. Since 1962 these championships have been held every four years.

An Olympic sport

Volleyball became an Olympic sport at the Tokyo Olympics in 1964. At Olympic level the men's gold medallists were Netherlands 1996 and Brazil 1992. Women's Olympic events have been dominated by Cuba who won gold in 1988, 1992 and 1996 in Atlanta.

What you need to play

The court

A volleyball match is usually played indoors on a timber-floored court measuring 18 metres by 9 metres. The 50-millimetre-wide boundary lines mark the edges of the court – any balls which hit the lines are considered 'in'. The court is divided into two equal sections by the **centre line**.

Above the centre line is the net which is one metre in depth and varies in height depending upon the age and sex of the players. The official height of the net, measured at its mid point, is 2.24 metres for women and 2.43 metres for men. The ends of the net may be up to two centimetres higher than the centre height. However, the net height can be reduced for skills practice, and for all but official games the net height doesn't need to be precise.

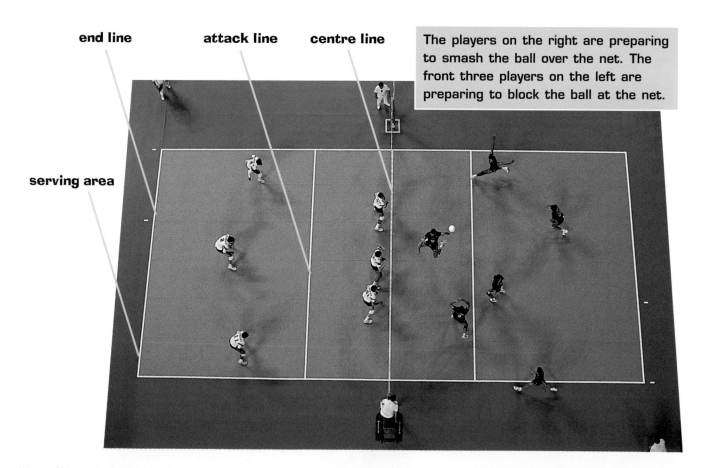

end line attack line centre line

serving area

The players on the right are preparing to smash the ball over the net. The front three players on the left are preparing to block the ball at the net.

Volleyball can be played on outdoor courts.

Across each half of the court there is an **attack line** which is located three metres from the net. The attack line divides each side of the court into a front zone (the **attack zone**) and a back zone. Only the three front court players on each team are permitted to smash the ball from within the attack zone. (Players from the back court may enter the attacking zone, but they may not play the ball from above the height of the net.)

The volleyball

The official volleyball is a light colour, 65–67 centimetres in circumference and weighs between 260 and 280 grams. Modified volleyballs are available for younger players. These softer balls are ideal for beginners as they allow the players to develop good handling techniques.

Clothing and shoes

Volleyball is played in shorts and a loose-fitting T-shirt. In competitions players in a team must all wear the same colour.

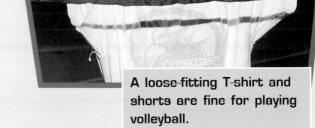

A loose-fitting T-shirt and shorts are fine for playing volleyball.

An all-purpose sports shoe is ideal for the beginner to intermediate level player. A thick sole (to provide cushioning) should provide good grip. The sole must be non-marking for indoor courts.

Knee pads

Players often **dive** for low balls and knee pads allow the player to retrieve low balls with a reduced risk of knee injury.

Rules

The object of the game of volleyball is to play the ball over the net and into the opponent's court by using any part of the body. The ball must be hit and never caught or held. Each team tries to play shots that their opponents will be unable to return.

Playing the ball

Each contact must give the ball immediate flight. The ball must be hit cleanly – it may not be **carried** (held for any length of time), lifted, scooped or thrown. The ball may be contacted with one hand or two, or any part of the body.

A team may contact the ball three times before it travels back over the net.

The block does not count as a contact.

The three-contact rule

A **contact** occurs whenever the ball touches a team member above or at waist height. Before returning the ball over the net, a team may contact the ball a maximum of three times. A fourth contact would result in a point to the other team or loss of service for the offending team. The ball may be legally hit back over the net with fewer than three contacts.

The only exception to the 'three-contact rule' occurs when a **block** at the net rebounds into the team's court. A block is a shot that attempts to stop a ball

coming over the net. The player jumps up at the net with both hands up to block the ball as it is smashed down across the net by a player on the other side. The block is not counted as a contact so the team is still allowed its three contacts.

Double hit

A **double hit** is illegal – no player may touch the ball twice in succession on his or her side of the net. The only exception to this rule occurs when the player first blocks the ball and then plays the ball again without a team-mate touching it in between.

Rules

Serving

Before the match begins the captains toss a coin for choice of 'side or serve'. The winning captain can choose to serve or to start the game from a preferred side of the court.

The player to commence serve stands behind the **end line**. The umpire blows a whistle, and the server has five seconds to play the ball. It is legal to serve underarm or overarm provided that the ball is struck cleanly with one hand only. The ball must be tossed into the air prior to being struck by the serving hand.

The serving player must:
- stand behind the end line
- strike the ball cleanly over the net, without touching it
- strike the ball so that it does not contact any of the server's team prior to its flight over the net. Only one attempt at service is allowed. If a serve is not successful, there is no change made to the score but the opposing team is awarded the service
- strike the ball so that it doesn't land outside the opponent's court.

Players must be careful not to touch or reach over the net as they play their shots.

Winning a point

A team wins a point when it has the service and the other team makes an error. These include:
- allowing the ball to touch the ground inside the court or on the boundary lines
- touching the ball more than the three permitted times before sending it back over the net
- hitting the ball over the net so that it lands on the other side, outside the opponent's court
- touching the net.

Side-out

Only the serving team can win a point – when the receiving team win a rally they do not score a point, but they do receive the serve. This is called a **side-out**.

Touching the opponent's court

No part of the body may completely cross the centre line to touch the opposite court. Your foot or hand may touch your opponent's court but some part of it must be in contact with the centre line.

Touching the net

The ball may not touch the net on service, but once the rally is in progress it is permitted to touch the net while crossing it. If the ball rebounds off the net, it may be played again only if the team has not already used its three contacts.

When a player's body or clothing touches the net a violation occurs. It is also illegal to pass the hand over the net to play a shot, unless the player is blocking a **spike** shot.

Ball in and out of bounds

The ball is 'in' if it lands anywhere on the court, including on any of the boundary lines. Even if the ball only touches the line slightly it is considered to be 'in'.

The ball is 'out' if it lands outside the court without touching the boundary lines, or if it touches the ceiling or an object outside the court. It is also 'out' if it hits the net without passing over it. If a ball is 'out' your opponents will score a point or your team will lose the service, depending on which team served the rally.

Substitutions

Each team may have up to six substitute players. Each team is permitted six substitutions in each set.

A player's foot may only cross the centre line into the opponent's court if some part of it is on the line.

Rules

Player positions

The teams spread themselves across the court so that the entire court is covered. The 'W formation' is usually used for receiving serve as it gives excellent coverage of the court.

- The centre front player (CF) stays at the net facing his team-mates.
- The centre back player (CB) stands in the centre of the back court.
- The front court players (RF and LF) cover the wide areas at mid-court.
- The right and left back players (RB and LB) cover their respective back corners.

Scoring

Three or five sets are played in a volleyball match. The winner is the team that wins the most sets.

When one team has won 15 points they have won a set – but they must have a lead of at least two points. If a game reaches a score of 14–14, play continues until one team gains a two-point lead or reaches 17 points. At the end of each set, teams change ends.

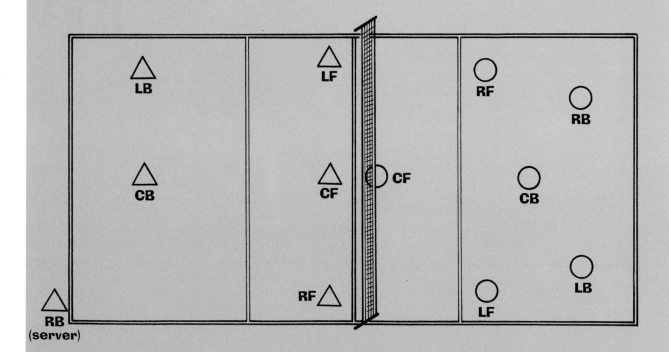

Serving team   Receiving team

Officials

A competition match is controlled by two officials. The referee, who is in charge of the game, sits on a stand to one side of the net. He decides whether a ball has been played legally or not, and when to award a point or a side-out (change of service).

The umpire stands at ground level opposite the referee. He or she controls substitutions, time outs, rotations and net offences.

Line judges assist the referee and the umpire to determine whether balls land in or outside the court.

Beginner-level matches are usually controlled by one umpire.

The attack zone

Once the ball is in play, the players may move around the court. However the three back court players are restricted in how they can play if they move into the attack zone (the front three metres of the court). When a back court player moves into the front court, he or she must not play the ball while it is above the height of the top of the net. In most cases this restricts these players to non-attacking shots in the front court.

Rotation

During a game each player will play in each of the six positions. The players rotate one position when the team regains the serve. While a team continues to win rallies the same server continues to serve and the players stay in their positions. When the team loses a rally a side-out occurs – the opponents take over the serve.

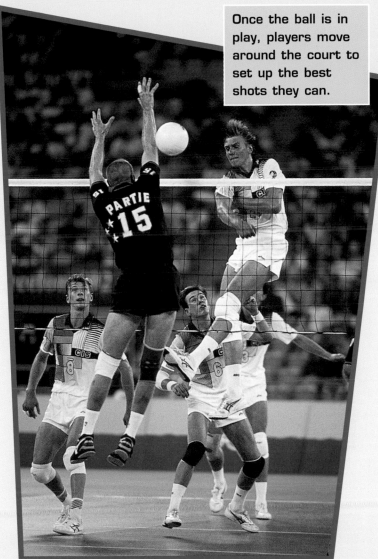

Once the ball is in play, players move around the court to set up the best shots they can.

The players of the new serving team rotate one position in a clockwise direction. The player who was in the right front (RF) position now takes the ball to serve.

Change of ends

Teams change ends after each set. They have a three-minute break between sets. If the match is taken to a fifth set, a coin is tossed to determine which team will serve first and from which end each team will play. In the fifth deciding set, the teams change ends when one of them reaches eight points.

Skills

There are two main areas of skills to learn to become a good volleyball player: serving and **passing** the ball. There are three serves and four main ways to pass the ball.

Serving:
- the underarm serve
- the overarm serve
- the **jump serve**

Passing the ball:
- the **dig**
- the **set**
- the spike

Serving

A serve commences each rally. With just one chance to serve the ball correctly, it is important to learn and practise this skill.

Underarm serve

Stand side-on to the net with your feet shoulder-width apart. Support the ball with your **platform hand**, the one closest to the net. Make a fist as you take your hitting hand back.

Move your weight to your front foot as you swing your hitting hand through. Drop your platform hand away from the ball just before striking it. Make contact with the ball in front of you at about waist height.

Hit the ball with the base of the palm of your hand. The ball should be at about waist height when you hit it. Follow through toward your target.

Underarm serve

The underarm serve should be mastered first. The ball travels over the net and into the opposite court in a high curve. It is an accurate and safe serve. The rules state that the ball must be hit cleanly with one hand only so be careful to keep your platform hand clear of the volleyball when your striking hand makes contact.

Overarm serve

The overarm serve is a powerful serve that puts the opponent under immediate pressure. Stand facing the net with one foot slightly forward. As you throw the ball up,

Make a fist as you take your arm straight back for the underarm serve.

bring your contact hand back behind your shoulder. Swing it powerfully forward as you step onto your front foot and hit the ball with a firm open hand.

Jump serve

The jump serve is an overarm serve where the server jumps up to strike the ball overhead while airborne. It can be used to give the serve more power, but should only be played once you have mastered the overarm serve.

The overarm serve action is similar in motion to the tennis serve.

Skills

Passing the ball

Passing the ball from one team-mate to another can be made with either a dig or a set.

Dig

The dig is normally used when receiving the ball from a service. The aim is to let the ball bounce cleanly on your forearms so that it travels in a high curve to a player at the front of the court.

As the ball approaches, move quickly to a position behind it with your knees bent and feet shoulder-width apart. Aim to contact the ball at or below waist level. For a low ball, bend your knees low to get down under it.

Place your arms so that the ball strikes your forearms just above the wrists. Bend your legs to absorb some of the ball's force to help you control its path. Straighten your legs after the ball bounces and follow through with your arms to about chin height.

Place the fingers of one hand across the fingers of your other and put your thumbs together. Contact is made with the forearms. A flat surface is essential as the ball is then unlikely to bounce off to the side.

With his knees bent and arms straight, this player is well-prepared to dig the ball safely to a team-mate.

Set

The set shot is played when the ball approaches from above head height. Its most common use is to set up for an attacking spike, but it is also ideal to send the ball long and high into an opponent's back court. It is generally the second shot in the three-contact sequence of play (see page 13).

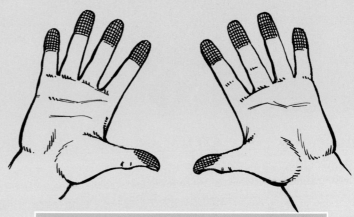

Contact with the ball should be made just above the forehead with the fingers of both hands cupped around and under the ball.

Move quickly into position with one leg in front of the other and your knees bent.

Bend your arms with your elbows outwards as you extend your hands above your head.

Straighten your legs and arms as you flick your wrists to power the ball away.

Skills

Spike

Sometimes called the smash, the spike is the most dynamic and attacking of all volleyball shots. Your aim is to smash the ball down hard into the opposite court. The spike is played from a position close to the net when the ball is high, usually when a team-mate has positioned it with a set.

Block

Most volleyball shots are attacking shots with the aim of setting up or executing winning shots. The block, however, is used to defend against the powerful spike. If players notice that their opponents are setting up a spike, they can prepare to defend by being ready to block the ball as it is hit down hard across the net.

When the ball is high and close to the net, jump as high as you can.

With an arm action like a tennis serve, strike the ball from above net height with a firm, cupped hand. Aim to project the ball down hard and fast into your opponent's court.

From a crouched position push off vertically with both feet. Your timing must be perfect and this will only be achieved with lots of practice.

An effective block turns a threatening spike into an attacking shot – possibly a point-winning shot.

The block is performed with both arms up, less than a ball-width apart, and your fingers spread to maximise the area used to block the ball. Sometimes a block can send the ball straight back to the opponent's side of the net. Other times it can deflect the ball over the player's head to his or her team-mates.

Dive

The dive can be used to **save** a very difficult ball. It is used when the ball is wide and out of range of the dig and involves diving for the ball to save it from bouncing. Once you have hit the ball, a team-mate can then keep the ball in play.

Push off one foot and jump or dive horizontally toward the ball. Play the ball from your forearm before landing. Once you have played the dive, move quickly back into position.

Skills

Team work

As well as practising the individual shots used in volleyball, it is important to practise sequences with your team. The usual sequence for the three contacts your team may have with the ball before it is sent back over the net is dig, set, spike.

The dig takes the force out of the ball as it is received from the opposing team and sends it high in the air towards the net.

The set receives the ball from the dig and springs it into the air close to the net, setting up the final contact.

A rally

1. The ball is hit over the net.

2. The ball is received with a dig shot that takes the pace off the ball and directs it to the attack zone at the front of the court.

3. The set shot puts the ball up in the attacking zone within about one metre of the net.

4. The ball is spiked by a leaping player who uses a powerful striking action to smash the ball over the net.

5. With outstretched arms and hands, a player on the opposing team tries to block the ball.

6. When the block is unsuccessful a team-mate may be able to dive to dig the ball up and back into play.

The spike powerfully smashes the ball into the opponent's court. It might be met with a block, or a dig, or it may hit the court resulting in a point for your team or a side-out, giving your team the serve.

If you are playing a dig shot, it is important to try to send the ball towards a player who is well-positioned to play a good set shot. Likewise, if you are playing a set shot, be aware of the player who will jump up to spike the ball. Plenty of practise with your team-mates will help you to anticipate where their shots will be placed and to know where best to place yours.

This sequence allows for a strong attacking shot to be played over the net to your opponents. However it is not compulsory to play a spike shot over the net. Until you are confident with the spike, the set shot can be played over the net.

Rallys

In a rally, the ball passes to and fro over the net any number of times before play is stopped by the ball hitting the ground or the net, or by illegal play. The illustration below shows a typical sequence of shots in a rally.

Beach volleyball

Beach volleyball has been an Olympic sport since the 1996 Olympic Games in Atlanta. It was first played on the beaches of southern California in the 1920s. Originally it was played in the traditional six-a-side format, but it was modified to a four-a-side game and then to the two-a-side game that it is today.

As the popularity of beach volleyball grew, the International Volleyball Federation promoted the World Beach Series, the World Indoor League and the European Grand Prix.

Rules

The rules of the standard game of volleyball have been adapted for the two-a-side beach game. The differences are:

- there are two players per team
- the ball is slightly heavier but softer, making it easier to control and less affected by the wind
- the game is played on sand

Players usually wear swimwear, often with hats and sunglasses, and they usually play in bare feet.

- there is no attack line and so no distinction between front court and back court players
- there is no centre line and players are allowed under the net as long as they don't interfere with their opponents
- teams change ends after every five points instead of after every set
- the court is the same size as for the standard game
- the boundary of the court is marked with ropes. The corners of the boundary are secured with anchors buried in the sand.
- the two players may stand anywhere on the court. Unlike the standard game of volleyball, players are not restricted to certain positions at the moment of service. When receiving a spike, one player usually stands ready to block at the net, while the other covers the rest of the court. When receiving serve each player stands in the back third of the court.
- players follow the rule of rotation as each player takes a turn at serving
- the ball may be held slightly when

Beach volleyball is a popular summertime sport.

setting, especially when it is being played from a difficult position or from a hard-hit attack
- a block shot is included as one of the team's three permitted contacts
- the service may only be received and played with a dig. The second hit is then used to set up your team-mate for the spike.

Getting ready

Always warm up your body before a match or practice session to minimise the risk of injury. Begin with running or jogging for a few minutes and then perform the stretches below.

Repeat each exercise four times on each side of the body. Hold each stretch for between 10 and 15 seconds and then relax the muscles before the next exercise.

Shoulder stretch
Stretch one arm straight across your body. Use your other hand to pull your elbow in to your chest until you feel the stretch.

Lower back stretch
Lie on your back with your legs outstretched. Bend one knee up to your chest and lift your head and shoulders off the floor to meet it. Lower yourself slowly back to the floor.

Arm and shoulder stretch
Bend your arm behind your head and gently push your elbow down with your other hand.

Inner thigh stretch
Stand with your feet wide apart and your toes pointing forwards. Rest your hands on one thigh and bend that knee. Keep your back straight and lean into your knee until you feel the stretch.

Arm circles
Stretch your arms above your head and then take them around in circles forwards and then backwards, stretching as far up and around as you can.

Calf stretch
Stand with one foot about one metre in front of the other. Bend your leading leg and lean forward, keeping both feet flat on the floor.

Quadricep stretch
Hold a wall, beam or a partner with one hand for balance. Bend one knee and pull your foot up behind you.

Side bends
Stand upright with one hand on your waist. Bring your other hand up over your head as you bend to the side. Make sure you don't lean forward as you bend.

Taking it further

Useful addresses

English Volleyball Association
27 South Road
West Bridgford
Nottingham
NG2 7AG
☎ 0115 981 6324
   0115 945 5429

(Further information could be gathered from the senior sports organisations below)

Sports Council
16 Upper Woburn Place
London
WC1H 0QP

CCPR
Francis House
Francis Street
London
SW1P 1DE

Further reading

Know the Game – Volleyball, A&C Black, London
Bulman, G. *Play the Game – Volleyball*, Blandford Publishers, London, 1992
Nicholls, K. *Volleyball – The Skills of the Game*, Crowood Press, Manborough, 1994

Glossary

attack line line dividing each side of the court into the attack zone and the back court. It is three metres from the centre line and parallel to it.

attack zone area of the court between the net and the attack line

back court the back six metres of the volleyball court

block a defensive move to prevent an attacking ball from coming over the net

carrying catching a ball, however slightly, before sending it up and back into play

centre line the line directly under the net which divides the court in two

contact whenever a player touches the ball

court the net, the boundary lines and the playing area

dig to recover a low ball by playing it with both your forearms under the ball.

dive a recovery of the ball when it is very low, by diving onto the court to get beneath it

double hit illegally hitting the ball twice in succession

end line the back boundary line of the court called the serve line

jump serve an overhead serve whereby the server strikes the ball while airborne

passing sending the ball from one team-mate to another

platform hand hand holding the ball just prior to service

rally a sequence of play in which the ball passes back and forth over the net several times before a point is scored

rotation each player moves clockwise to the next position when their team gains service

save preventing a low ball from hitting the court

serve to bring the ball into play at the start of each new rally. The serve is hit directly over the net from behind the end line.

set shot played to set the ball up for the spiker to smash it over the net. The set is played with the fingertips.

set part of a match. A set is won when one team reaches 15 points.

side-out change of service. When the team receiving serve wins a rally, they don't add a point to their score, but they gain service.

spike a very forceful, attacking shot where the ball is hit down across the net

volley a shot where the ball is played before it bounces. In volleyball, every legal shot is a volley.

Index